a visit to Mackinac Island

by Jen Tucker

illustrated by
Jennifer Powell

For Kylie and Trevor
who love sandcastles almost as much as I do.

–JT

For Mike who chose Mackinac Island as a backdrop
when he asked me to be his bride.

–JP

Illustrated by Jennifer Powell

Printed in the United States of America

First Printing, 2016

ISBN 978-1-945091-09-4

Ordering Information: Special discounts are available on quantity purchases by bookstores, corporations, associations, and others. For details, contact the publisher at sales@braughlerbooks.com or at 937-58-BOOKS.

For questions or comments about this book, please write to info@braughlerbooks.com.

Braughler
Books
braughlerbooks.com

"Mom, Patsy and Clyde are waiting for me on Mackinac Island, so let's shake a tail feather!" Ella said impatiently. Her favorite place to visit was only a short ferry ride away.

"We'll see them soon," Mom reminded her. Waiting was not Ella's strong suit.

The captain requested her ticket. "I'm visiting friends on the island today," she said.

"I'll do my best to get you there as fast as I can," he said with a wink.

Ella spied out the misty window.

Crewmen scurried. Parasails launched. Fishermen celebrated.

Upon arrival, Ella was first to disembark.

Main Street overflowed with visitors. Some followed maps, while others window shopped.

"Time to rent bikes," said Dad.

"Are you sure?" Ella asked, smelling sweet treats from the store across the way. "I'm pretty sure it's ice cream first, then rent bikes."

Unfortunately for Ella, that was not the order of events.

Butter pecan for Dad. Chocolate chip mint for Mom. Bubble gum for Ella.

Finding a grassy spot along the waterfront, they sat and enjoyed the view.

Seagulls swooped. Lilacs bloomed. Horses trotted. What a beautiful day.

One of Ella's favorite stops was next—
the butterfly gardens. Inside, butterflies
flitted freely.

Monarchs ate milkweed. Chrysalises grew.
Three Swallowtails landed on Dad.

"They must love my bald head."
He laughed.

Cycling through town, Ella noticed the general store. "Wait!" she cried while slowing her bike. "I need to buy something *special* for some special *someones*."

Jingling the coins in her pocket, Ella entered the store.

She returned and let Mom peek inside the bag. "I bought a surprise for Patsy and Clyde."

Mom smiled. "They'll love it," she said.

After zooming down the big hill, Ella stopped her bike. She parked it against the barn.

Patsy and Clyde's ears perked up. They watched Ella walk toward them.

She patted their heads. "I missed you, you beautiful horses. Did you miss me?" she asked.

She opened the bag. One apple for Patsy and one apple for Clyde.

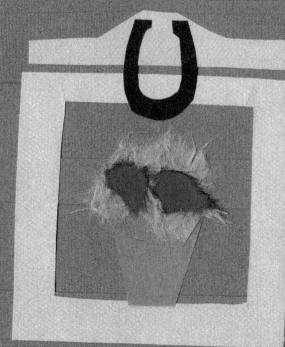

"Are you ready for a carriage ride, Ella?" Miss Molly asked. She patted the seat next to her. "This year you're old enough to help me drive."

"I knew there were perks to growing up," she replied.

The carriage cruised along the streets of Mackinac Island. Birds chirped. Trees towered overhead. People waved.

They came to a stop alongside the Grand Hotel porch. Ella observed the stately homes and cozy cottages lining the bluff. "One day, I'm going to live in one of those houses," she confidently claimed.

"Me too. Can I be your roommate?" asked Miss Molly.

"Not if you snore," she replied.

Before too long, the ride ended where it began. "How'd I do, Miss Molly?" Ella asked.

"You're a natural," she replied. "Same time next year?"

Ella stroked the horses' manes. "I wouldn't miss it for the world."

The End.

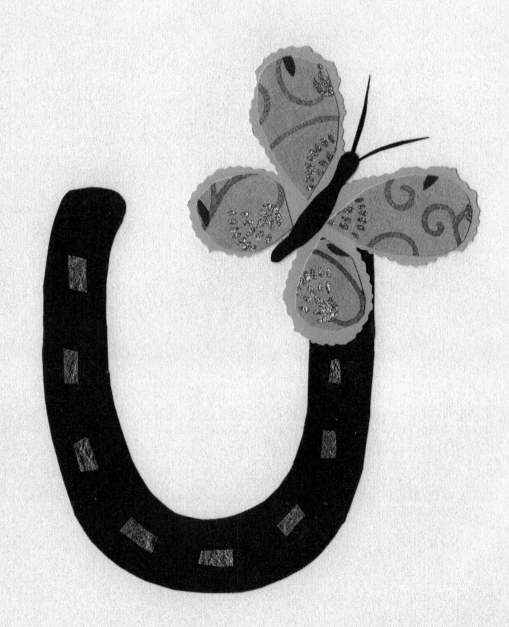

Jen Tucker has never met a gluten free cupcake she didn't like. When she isn't penning commercials, short films, books, and columns you can find her spending time with her ever-patient husband and three moxie-filled children at their home in Indiana. Jen has spent many summers on the shores of the Great Lakes epically failing to learn the art of skipping stones.

Jennifer Powell has a lifelong love of art, education and the outdoors. Jennifer has a BA in education from Michigan State University and an MA from Eastern Michigan University. She has written and illustrated several children's books. Jennifer lives in Mackinac County, Michigan with her husband and two sons. She had an American Saddlebred horse, named Taffy, when she was Ella's age.

CPSIA information can be obtained
at www.ICGtesting.com
Printed in the USA
LVOW05s1145090816
499562LV00026B/201/P